The Naked Mole-Rat

by Jody Rake

Consulting Editor: Gail Saunders-Smith, PhD

Consultant: Rochelle Buffenstein, PhD
Barshop Institute for Aging and Longevity Studies
University of Texas Health Science Center
San Antonio, Texas

Capstone
press

Mankato, Minnesota

Pebble Plus is published by Capstone Press,
1710 Roe Crest Drive, North Mankato, Minnesota 56003.
www.capstonepub.com

082014
008384R

 Books published by Capstone Press are manufactured with paper
containing at least 10 percent post-consumer waste.

Library of Congress Cataloging-in-Publication Data
Rake, Jody Sullivan.
    The naked mole-rat / by Jody Rake.
    p. cm. — (Pebble plus. Weird animals)
    Includes bibliographical references and index.
    Summary: "Simple text and photos describe the unique homes, bodies, behaviors and
adaptations of naked mole-rats" — Provided by publisher.
    ISBN-13: 978-1-4296-1739-0 (hardcover)
    ISBN-10: 1-4296-1739-X (hardcover)
    1. Naked mole rat — Juvenile literature. I. Title. II. Series.
QL737.R628R35 2009
599.35'9 — dc22   2008003897

Editorial Credits
Jenny Marks, editor; Ted Williams and Kyle Grenz, designers; Wanda Winch, photo researcher

Photo Credits
Alamy/blickwinkel, 7; Phototake Inc., 11
AnimalsAnimals/Raymond Mendez, 15
Corbis/dpa/Wolfgang_Thieme, 19
Nature Picture Library/Neil Bromhall, 9, 12–13
Peter Arnold/R. Andrew Odum, cover
SuperStock, Inc./ZSSD, 1
Visuals Unlimited/ Jennifer Jarvis, 16–17; Justin O'Riain, 4–5; M. J. O'Riain & J. Jarvis, 20–21

Note to Parents and Teachers

The Weird Animals series supports national science standards related to life science.
This book describes and illustrates naked mole-rats. The images support early readers
in understanding the text. The repetition of words and phrases helps early readers learn
new words. This book also introduces early readers to subject-specific vocabulary words,
which are defined in the Glossary section. Early readers may need assistance to read
some words and to use the Table of Contents, Glossary, Read More, Internet Sites, and
Index sections of the book.

Table of Contents

Wrinkly Rodents

What is that

pink, wrinkly animal?

It is a rodent

called a naked mole-rat.

Naked mole-rats live
in northeast Africa.
Their strange bodies
are perfect for their homes.

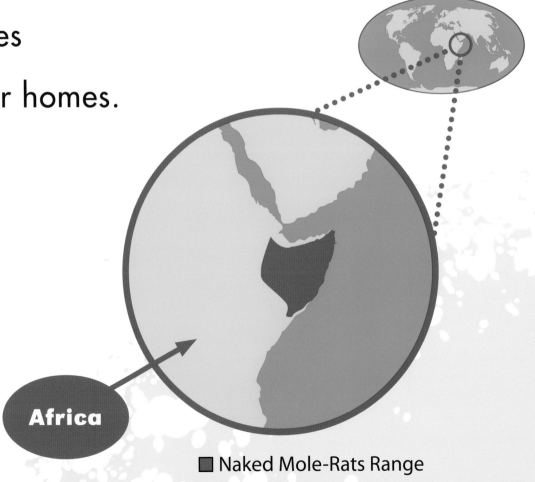

Africa

■ Naked Mole-Rats Range

Living in the Dark

Naked mole-rats live

in underground burrows.

They dig the burrows

with long, curved teeth.

Naked mole-rats' eyes
are almost blind.
Their whiskers
help them feel around
in the dark.

Finding Food

Munch!

Naked mole-rats eat roots.

They dig all day

to find food.

Hungry snakes eat
naked mole-rats.

They sneak into burrows.

Watch out, naked mole-rats!

The Life of Naked Mole-Rats

Naked mole-rats live in family groups called colonies.

Only one female has babies. She is called the queen.

Naked mole-rats live

about 20 years.

They live even longer in zoos.

Have you seen one in a zoo?

Naked mole-rats have
weird body parts.
But their bodies are perfect
for where they live.

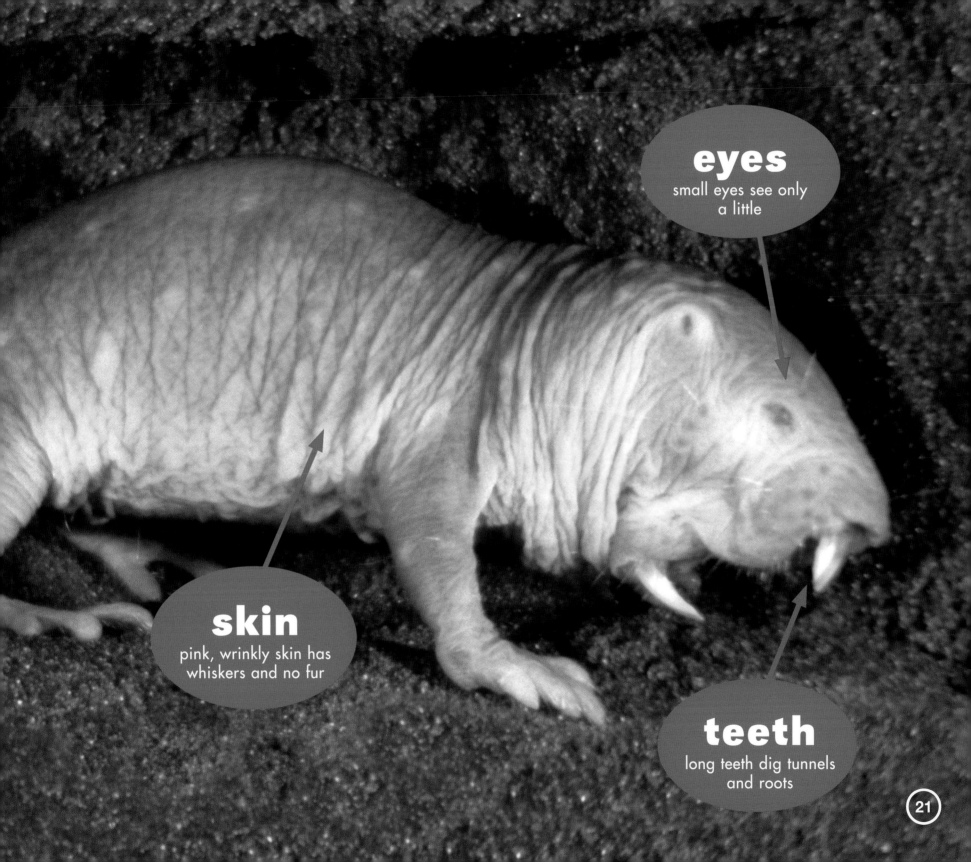

eyes
small eyes see only
a little

skin
pink, wrinkly skin has
whiskers and no fur

teeth
long teeth dig tunnels
and roots

21

Glossary

blind — unable to see

burrow — a home in a tunnel dug underground; naked mole-rats live in burrows.

colony — a group of animals that live together; naked mole-rats live in colonies.

rodent — a member of a group of mammals with long front teeth for gnawing

whisker — a long, stiff hair; naked mole-rats use their whiskers to feel.

wrinkly — covered with creases or lines; naked mole-rats have wrinkly skin.

Read More

Gerstein, Sherry. *Animal Planet: the Most Extreme Animals.* San Francisco: Jossey-Bass, 2007.

Martin, Patricia A. Fink. *Naked Mole-Rats.* Nature Watch. Minneapolis: Carolrhoda Books, 2003.

Internet Sites

FactHound offers a safe, fun way to find Internet sites related to this book. All of the sites on FactHound have been researched by our staff.

Here's how:

1. Visit *www.facthound.com*

2. Choose your grade level.

3. Type in this book ID **142961739X** for age-appropriate sites. You may also browse subjects by clicking on letters, or by clicking on pictures and words.

4. Click on the **Fetch It** button.

FactHound will fetch the best sites for you!

Index

Word Count: 134
Grade: 1
Early-Intervention Level: 20